Enrich Your Life

World's Classics

100 Greatest Novels of All Time

www.iboo.com

I'M ON THE SAME PAGE

CREATIVE EDGE PUBLICITY

Your brand. Your future.

+1 403-464-6925
www.creative-edge.services

Save
The Ocean

Feed
The World

OCEANA

Restoring the oceans could feed 1 billion people a healty seafood meal each day

10 ON THE COVER

On our cover is acclaimed and Award-Winning Author Weam Namou who is the Executive Director of the Chaldean Cultural Center, which houses the first and only Chaldean Museum in the world. She's an Eric Hoffer award-winning author of 14 books, an international award-winning filmmaker, journalist, poet, and an Ambassador for the Authors Guild of America [Detroit Chapter], the nation's oldest and largest writing organization. She hosts a half-hour weekly TV show, and she's the founder of The Path of Consciousness, a spiritual and writing community, and Unique Voices in Films, a nonprofit organization

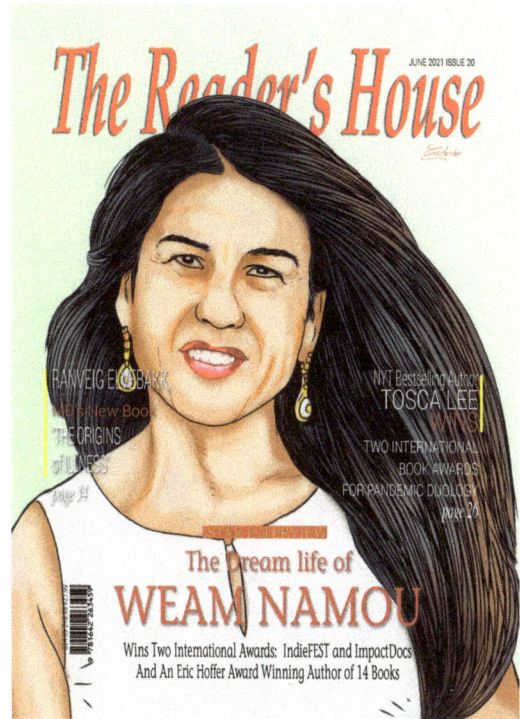

The Reader's House

JUNE 2021 ISSUE 20

RANVEIG ELVEBAKK
MD's New Book
"THE ORIGINS
of ILLNESS"

NYT Bestselling Author
TOSCA LEE
WINS
TWO INTERNATIONAL
BOOK AWARDS
FOR PANDEMIC DUOLOGY

The Dream life of
WEAM NAMOU
Wins Two International Awards: IndieFEST and ImpactDocs
And An Eric Hoffer Award Winning Author of 14 Books

In this Issue

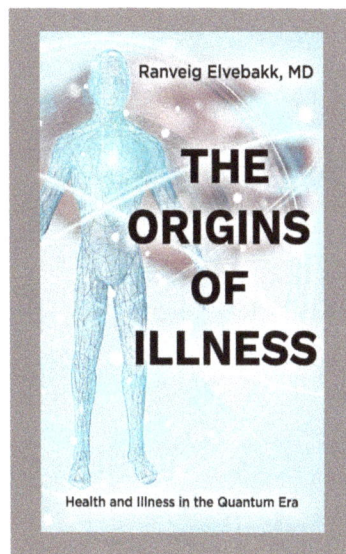

Ranveig Elvebakk, MD

THE
ORIGINS
OF
ILLNESS

Health and Illness in the Quantum Era

34 BOOK

Ranveig Elvebakk, MD, a Scandinavian-born medical doctor, and fitness advocate, has completed her most recent book "THE ORIGINS OF ILLNESS: Health and Illness in the Quantum Era": a potent analysis on how the physical environment and the human body affect each other. It studies the body's response to the changing planet and allows readers to understand this relationship in order to come to a symbiosis, subsequently preventing illnesses and diseases.

14 BOOKS PRAISE

my pursuit of beauty

by VINCE SPINNATO
ISBN: 978-1610059640
PUBLISHER: BookLogix

22 Author Lorenza Fontenot's New Book

Scandalous Jazmynn' is a Psychological Romantic Murder Mystery About a Scandal

38 HEALTH

Personal Experience of Colorectal Cancer is an Irreverent, Cheeky Tail of Surviving, Thriving and Transforming Through Illness

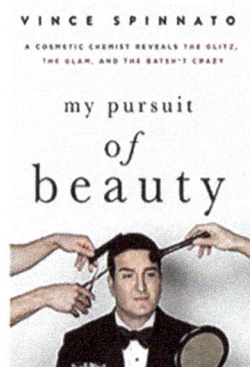

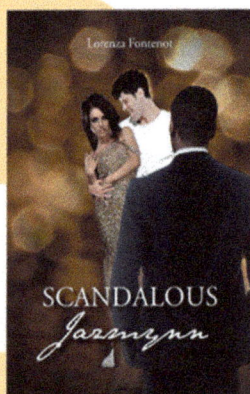

EDITOR'S LETTER

The thing I admire most about the award-winning authors featured in this magazine is that they are good at their jobs. Really, they are just good at life. Weam Namou is one of them. She is a mom who love her children as well as community advocates who embrace the region.

On our cover is acclaimed and Award-Winning Author **Weam Namou** who is the Executive Director of the Chaldean Cultural Center, which houses the first and only Chaldean Museum in the world. She's an Eric Hoffer award-winning author of 14 books, an international award-winning filmmaker, journalist, poet, and an Ambassador for the Authors Guild of America [Detroit Chapter], the nation's oldest and largest writing organization. She hosts a half-hour weekly TV show, and she's the founder of The Path of Consciousness, a spiritual and writing community, and Unique Voices in Films, a nonprofit organization.

We continue to connect people who are always ready to share their story and passion with an interview, and we put them to The Reader's House spotlight. We have interviewed not just acclaimed, as well as award winning authors like *Jennifer Anne Gordon*, a gothic horror/literary fiction novelist, won the Kindle Award for Best Horror/Suspense for 2020, Won Best Horror 2020 from Authors on the Air, was a Finalist for American Book Fest's Best Book Award- Horror, 2020. She also received the Platinum 5 Star Review from Reader's Choice as well as the Gold Seal from Book View.

We featured Enlightened Thought Leader *Dr. Chérie Carter-Scott* on the cover of March issue. *Dr Chérie* is #1 New York Times Best Selling Author (19 Books), Oprah Winfrey Endorsed, Consultant to Fortune 500 companies.

International Bestselling Author *Kathrin Hutson*, NY Times Bestseller Author *Tosca Lee*, Acclaimed crime fiction Canadian Author, *Melissa Yi*, Past President of the Sisters In Crime NJ and Award Winning Author, *Kristina Rienzi* are some of authors we will feature on the cover in upcoming issues.

Enjoy Reading

A. Harlowe

The Reader's House

Published by Newyox

LONDON OFFICE
3rd Floor
86-90 Paul Street
London
EC2A 4NE UK

t: +44 20 3828 7097
editor@newyox.com
newyox.com

Editor in Chief
Anna Harlowe

Managing Director
Dan Peters

Marketing Director
Ben Alan

Cover Art
Murat Sevinc

CONTRIBUTORS

Mickey Mikkelson
Andy Machin
Rocky Cole
Jean Taylor
Rosina S Khan
Shalini M
Anders Abadie
Vinod Vullikanti
Hannah SPRAKER

Due to the current lockdown in England, we are working remotely until further notice. Currently, we are still producing publications; should this change, we will contact any customers this affects. This means our phones have been turned off and we're currently only available by email (editor@newyox.com). We will be answering emails as quickly as possible and we thank you in advance for your patience and understanding. We'll keep our website updated as and when things change.

We assume no responsibility for unsolicited manuscripts or art materials.

The Dream life of
WEAM NAMOU

Wins Two International Awards: IndieFEST and ImpactDocs
And An Eric Hoffer Award Winning Author of 14 Books

"Despite the large population of Arab Americans (roughly 3.5 million), our stories are underrepresented, marginalized, and stereotypical. This is partly due to the Arab/Chaldean-American community not providing a strong enough vehicle to develop and encourage the arts, which results in the perpetuation of the patriarchal stereotype."

BY DAN PETERS

May 15, 2021

Born in Baghdad to an ancient lineage called the Chaldeans, Weam Namou is the Executive Director of the Chaldean Cultural Center, which houses the first and only Chaldean Museum in the world. She's an Eric Hoffer award-winning author of 14 books, an international award-winning filmmaker, journalist, poet, and an Ambassador for the Authors Guild of America [Detroit Chapter], the nation's oldest and largest writing organization. She hosts a half-hour weekly TV show, and she's the founder of The Path of Consciousness, a spiritual and writing community, and Unique Voices in Films, a nonprofit organization.

What's the last great book you read?

Hillbilly Elegy by J.D. Vance

What's your favorite book no one else has heard of?

Daughter of Fire: A Diary of a Spiritual Training with a Sufi Master
This is the diary of Irina Tweedie, the first ever western (British) woman to be trained in the Naqshbandiyya-Mujad-didiyya Sufi Order lineage. It spans five years, and reveals her spiritual transformation in India. When she returned to England, she started a small Sufi mediation group in North Lond and later named Llewellyn Vaughan-Lee as her successor to continue her work after she retired in 1992.

Are there any classic novels that you only recently read for the first time?

Charlotte Bronte's Jane Eyre

You're organizing a party. Which two authors, dead or alive, do you invite?

1.   Enheduanna, the first recorded writer in history (2285-2250 BCE). The daughter of Sargon the Great, she was a princess, priestess, and poet in ancient Mesopotamia, and has been called the Shakespeare of Sumerian literature. She was the first to sign her name to her poetry, something never done before. Therefore, she made her permanent mark on history by composing, in her own name, a series of more than 40 extraordinary liturgical works which were copied for nearly 2,000 years.
2.   Maria Theresa Asmar – Born in 1804, Maria was a Chaldean Catholic from Tel Keppe in northern Iraq, the village where my parents and grandparents

Continued *on page 16*

"I was born in Baghdad to an indigenous people called the Chaldeans, Neo-Babylonians who still speak Aramaic. My family fled Saddam's regime and we immigrated to the United States in February 1981, when I was ten years old. My parents, my father in particular, encouraged me to acclimate to my new country, and that gave me a strong foundation to pursue the American dream." W. NAMOU

COVER IMAGE (PAINT) BY MURAT SEVINC
KURTIS ZETOUNA (B/W)

It's time to take a stand for homeless pets. It's time to adopt change. Every day, more than 4,100 dogs and cats are killed in shelters across the country — but **with Best Friends Animal Society leading the way, and your support, we can help our nation's shelters and Save Them All**

SAVE
THEM
ALL

my pursuit of beauty

by VINCE SPINNATO
ISBN: 978-1610059640
PUBLISHER: BookLogix

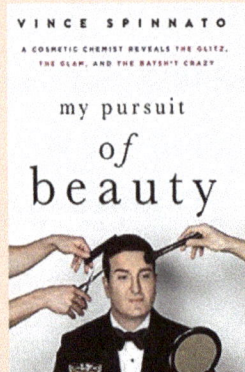

'Dynasty, ' produced by my dad, Aaron Spelling, sparked the imagination of my friend, Vince Spinnato, and inspired him to turn his dreams of developing luxury beauty products into a reality. His no-holds-barred memoir describing his struggles to the top is brutally honest, hilarious and heartbreaking. I couldn't put the book down." -**Tori Spelling, actress/author of "sTori Telling"**

"Vince's honesty and his scientific talent about the skincare industry has made me love this book and his products. Growing up with the legendary iconic faces of MGM royalty like my mother, Judy Garland, I understand the trust you need to have in today's confusing billion-dollar beauty industry. When you find the right 'wizard' you are grateful and stay connected." **-Lorna Luft, singer/actor, "The New York Times" bestselling author of "A Star is Born: The Film That Got Away" and five-time Emmy award-winning producer of the mini- series "Judy Garland: Me and My Shadow"**

"As a beauty professional and founder of the largest 'meeting and discussing' book club in the world, I knew from the first chapter that this was from a perspective of creating 'beauty' that I had not read before. I flew through the pages. Five Diamonds in the Pulpwood Queen Recommended Reading list. This dazzling gem is the Official 2021 February Pulpwood Queen/Timber Guys Book of the Month Club Selection!" **-Kathy L. Murphy, founder of International Pulpwood Queens and Timber Guys Book Reading Nation and author of "The Pulpwood Queen's Tiara Wearing, Book Sharing Guide to Life**

SCORPION SCHEME

by MELISSA YI
ISBN: 978-1927341872
PUBLISHER: Olo Books

"**ER meets Homeland in a frenetic** Egyptian adventure. Hope Sze turns her medical crimefighting into an international incident. Terrorism, tombs, sarcasm, and sex."—Dr. Frank Warsh, author of Hippocrates: the Art and the Oath

"**Scorpion Scheme is to**p-notch historical crime fiction with a fabulous kick-ass female protagonist. The kind of book that you just can't put down. Scorpion Scheme is Robin Cook meets D.J. McIntosh's fabulous Mesopotamian trilogy but it delivers a stingingly good tale all on its own steam."—Lisa de Nikolits, author of The Rage Room

#1 Mystery Selection—CBC Books, on Human Remains. Recommended authors also include Louise Penny and Maureen Jennings

One of the best Canadian suspense books recommended by Margaret Cannon, The Globe and Mail, on Human Remains

"**Smart and sassy.**"—Jim Napier, Reviewing the Evidence

WINTER ROAD

by KRISTINA RIENZI

ISBN: 978-0996972123
PUBLISHER: Indigo Hawk Group

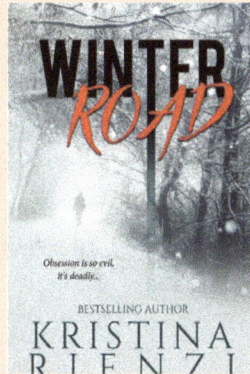

What Readers Said about Winter Road:

"Loved this book. It started straight away with love excitement,thrill. This book kept you reading till the end. I would recommend this book."

"A grip your seat quick read!"

"Well this was quite an action packed little gem! You know a book is good when immediately upon finishing it - you head over to Amazon and add every other book the author has written to your wish list! This story puts you on the edge of your seat every page of the way with its excellent character development and very suspenseful, exciting plot. A quick, easy read, but well worth it. Trust me, if you are a mystery or suspense fan, you don't want to miss this one!"

"WOW! What a great quick read! Kristina Rienzi will keep you on suspense, the pages kept turning to see what was going to happen next!"

Wuthering Heights

by Emily Brontë
ISBN: 978-1641814140

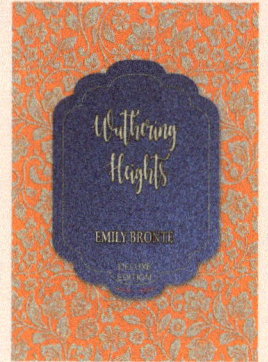

James Lorimer
"Here all the faults of Jane Eyre (by Charlotte Brontë) are magnified a thousand fold, and the only consolation which we have in reflecting upon it is that it will never be generally read."

"as a whole, it is wild, confused, disjointed, and improbable; and the people who make up the drama, which is tragic enough in its consequences, are savages ruder than those who lived before the days of Homer."
Anonymous

"Wuthering Heights is a strange, inartistic story. There are evidences in every chapter of a sort of rugged power—an unconscious strength—which the possessor seems never to think of turning to the best advantage."
Anonymous

"it's my absolute favorite book and I have searched and searched for a movie version that captured it accurately." KrazyFotoFreak

⬅ **Continued** *from page 10*

were born. Unfortunately, the village was destroyed in 2014 when ISIS invaded the area. Maria traveled to the Middle East and Europe on her own, and wrote Memoirs of a Babylonian Princess, which consists of two volumes and 720 pages. She met with Queen Victoria in England, who sponsored her book, and even dedicated her book to the Queen.

Who are your favorite writers? Are there any who aren't as widely known as they should be, whom you'd recommend in particular?

Lynn V. Author, bestselling author of the Medicine Woman series which consists of over 20 books. Lynn also teaches mys-

"After I graduated from Wayne State University with a Bachelor's in Speech Communication, I started traveling the world while keeping journals and attempting to write my first book."

ticism, through classes and her books. I studied with Lynn for four years, and for a number of years, I've been a mentor for her apprentices.

What do you read when you're working on a book? And what kind of reading do you avoid while writing?

When I'm working on a book, I mostly read material that serves as research. I also read books that resemble the genre I'm working on. For instance, if I'm writing a memoir, I read memoir to get a sense of how an author used his or her voice to tell their story.

What moves you most in a work of literature?

The things that move me in a work of literature are honestly, simplicity, humor, and the ability to use language colorfully to bring characters, settings, and dialogue to life. When an author's voice is pure and genuine, they don't need to rely on a plot to get you from one page to the next. The quality and heart of their words does that in itself.

What genres do you especially enjoy reading?

For a very long time now, I've really enjoyed reading nonfiction books, especially memoirs and biographies. Real people

intrigue me, and I find that reading about the life of others is both entertaining as well as a great way to learn something, feel motivated, and get a new perspective.

Who is your favorite fictional hero or heroine?

Scarlett O'Hara. The first book I ever read was Gone with the Wind, in Arabic! I was nine years old and living in Amman, Jordan, with my family as we awaited a visa to come to the United States. As non-residents, my younger brother and I weren't allowed to go to school in Jordan. I loved books and this one was lying around, so I gobbled it up. I loved Scarlett and her tribe, and despite our differences, I was able to connect to her. My family saw how carried I was by this book, so they took me to the movies for the very first time in my life to watch Gone with the Wind, with Arabic subtitles. Imagine a nine-year-old girl from Baghdad, Iraq being able to relate to a Southern teenage girl from Georgia. The two were worlds apart, but Mitchell's storytelling transcended our differences through the common human traits we all have of love, fear, family, and desire. That's how I would describe my work. It's good storytelling that takes readers along a journey they might have never gone on before but which they can as human beings relate and connect to.

That story was my pre-introduction to America, so needless to say, there was quite a culture shock when I arrived to the United States and found no sign of horse carriages, of women wearing fancy puffy dresses, families having extravagant barbecues followed by extravagant drawn-out naps. George in 1860s was not Michigan in the 1980s!

What books and authors have impacted your writing career?

The classics impacted my writing career, such as Henry James' Washington Square, Gustave Flaubert's Madame Bovary, of course Margaret Mitchell's Gone with the Wind, and many others. Classic authors had an excellence in the craft of storytelling. They didn't rely on impressing the reader with off-beat techniques, political drama, sexuality, violence, and other topics that are often thrown in just to grab one's attention. My first New York agent, Frances Kuffel, said that my work had the style of Jane

Austen. An Iraqi critic mentioned the same in a review of my first book, The Feminine Art. Like Austen, my books are about typical people in everyday life.

What kind of reader were you as a child?

In Baghdad, Iraq, we basically read whatever the school required of us to read. As early as first grade, schools started students with mostly text books.

Tell us about yourself and your company, What kind of Corporation is your business?

I was born in Baghdad to an indigenous people called the Chaldeans, Neo-Babylonians who still speak Aramaic. My family fled Saddam's regime and we immigrated to the United States in February 1981, when I was ten years old. My parents, my father in particular, encouraged me to acclimate to my new country, and that gave me a strong foundation to pursue the American dream.

After I graduated from Wayne State University with a Bachelor's in Speech Communication, I started traveling the world while keeping journals and attempting to write my first book. I studied novel, nonfiction, and memoir writing through various years-long correspondences courses (this was before the internet). I studied poetry in Prague through the University of New Orleans Prague Summer Program, filmmaking at MPI (Motion Picture Institute of Michigan) and learned the sacred art of living through the most powerful spiritual teachers, including a man from India named Narendra, a Native American man and his partner (Chip and Susan), and most recently from bestselling author and mystic, Lynn V. Andrews.

Unable to find stories of my people and culture anywhere, I took refuge in western literature and films until I took up pen and paper and started to write about my Iraqi American experiences. To find my own voice and write authentic stories of my heritage, I had to find my own opportunities so as not to cave into the pressures of the publishing and film industry which wanted me to write stories that fit into their definition of diversity. As a woman of Middle Eastern background, this was especially important for me. It meant writing what I knew, in a fascinating way, without having to rely on wars, violence, the abuse and oppression of women, and other stereotypical dramas associated with the people and culture of the Middle East. It meant that my children and the younger generation, in general, will have the chance to view a version of themselves that's relatable and inspirational rather than pigeonholed. Over the decades, I was still unable to find stories of my people anywhere, so I tried to fill that void. I founded Hermiz Publishing, Inc. in 2004 and not long after graduating from MPI, a one-year full-time film school, I founded my production company, Namou Productions, Inc. In 2018, I founded Unique Voices in Films, a 501 (C)(3) nonprofit organization.

What is unique about your business?

Despite the large population of Arab Americans (roughly 3.5 million), our stories are underrepresented, marginalized, and stereotypical. This is partly due to the Arab/Chaldean-American community not providing a strong enough vehicle to develop and encourage the arts, which results in the perpetuation of the patriarchal stereotype.

Another reason why our voices are not heard is that the same institutions that claim they want "diverse and unique voices" have their own version of diver-

"My businesses break barriers, providing authentic stories of my people and culture that you cannot find in other books, films, or in television. Today most stories about Iraq, or the Arab World in general, have to do with violence, war, and politics. The beautiful, loving, and witty side of the people and culture of that region is rarely brought forth."

sity and uniqueness.

My businesses break barriers, providing authentic stories of my people and culture that you cannot find in other books, films, or in television. Today most stories about Iraq, or the Arab World in general, have to do with violence, war, and politics. The beautiful, loving, and witty side of the people and culture of that region is rarely brought forth. I feel that it's my responsibility to share such stories given that I live in Michigan, which has the largest population of Iraqi born residents and the largest concentration of Arab Americans in the United States.

How and why did you get started in this line of work?

Being a storyteller is my calling. Focusing on Iraqi American stories is my passion, inspiration and my expertise. The older I become, the more I understand the importance of documenting through literature and film these stories, especially that of the Chaldeans, an ancient group in danger of facing extinction. Chaldeans trace their roots to Ur, land of the Chaldees in southern Mesopotamia. They contributed a great deal to the building of the cradle of civilization, where writing, the wheel, city-states, and many "firsts" were invented. Unfortunately, due to centuries of wars, persecution, oppression, and violence – most recently the spread of ISIS forces – the community is now in diaspora and its cultural identity endangered. So my commitment to this line of work keeps growing.

How do you deal with the stress of Covid-19? What was the worst part of business since the covid-19 started? How covid-19 affected the way of doing business?

Since October 2019, I've been the executive director of the Chaldean Cultural Center, which houses the world's first and only Chaldean museum. Before COVID, I worked at the office in the daytime four days a week. I came home shortly after my two children were home from school, set up dinner which I often prepared before leaving the house, and we usually ate together once my husband was home. After the kitchen was cleared, in the late evening, I worked on my writing and film projects. I also saved my weekends for personal work and family time.

Since March 2020, it was difficult to have a routine or sane schedule. My work hours increased, and there were no boundaries between weekdays and weekends, daytime and nighttime. My children were learning from home and requiring additional attention. It was a challenge convincing them this wasn't vacation time! And it was nearly impossible to unplug from the phone, computer, Zoom meetings, etc.

But I did notice that I was able to accomplish a lot more. It was just a matter of adjusting to the new routine. It was overwhelming, however, trying to make these new decisions on a daily basis, and not knowing what to expect with the world's health situation. The emotional aspect to all this is really another story, one that I'm undergoing especially right now. Recently I was diagnosed with COVID pneumonia and admitted to the hospital. It was surprising to me and the doctors, given I have no health issues whatsoever and am on no medications. My only visits to the doctor are for a routine yearly checkup. Thank God, all turned out okay, but the experience was scary and the pandemic has caused me to once again pause and think about the future.

What was the best part of your work?

Being able to do what I love while taking care of my home and family.

How do you advertise your business?

I have a publicist, and I a strong team who helps me strategize different ways to reach my goals and audience.

To what do you attribute your success?

Working hard, persistence, belief in myself, and faith in God.

What's your company's goals?

To continue producing quality work on a consistent basis.

Where do you see yourself in five years?

I see myself doing the same type of work, but reaching a much larger audience, and being in a position to help many more people to reach their dreams.

If you had one piece of advice to someone just starting out, what would it be?

Believe in yourself long enough to see the project through to the end. Be patient. Don't use your gender, marital status, parenthood, money, or any other factor as an excuse for not honoring your dreams and aspirations. Don't be afraid to work hard. Be creative as well as practical so that you don't rely on connections, philosophy, dreams, and luck to get you where you want to go. Your faith, work, and persistence will communicate to the universe your needs, and somehow, somewhere, the things you want the most will happen. ●

Vist weamnamou.com to learn more about Weam Namou and and her works.

Books do not market themselves, nor do agents and publishers do all the work for you if you've gone that route. And if you're a self-published author, that means most or all of the burden of marketing falls upon your shoulders.

This article talks about methods you can use to promote your book. One thing I want to point out is that it's difficult to determine which methods pay off even after you've made them. Sometimes book sales can happen as a result of a combination of two or more different methods, and even after the fact, you may not know which methods played a role.

Most of these approaches are free, except for your time, so I say, try as many of them as you can.

Book Promotion and Marketing

BY FLORENCE OSMUND

MARKETING PLAN

It is advisable to have a marketing plan before you start, even if it's a simple plan that evolves over time. Consider the following elements:

• Set goals for yourself -- establish a number for the number of books you want to sell, earnings, number of books written, number of author interviews you do, number of guest blogs you partici- pate in, Amazon ranking, number of hits on your website, number of Facebook "likes," number of articles you write, and number of positive reviews you get.

• Know your target audience. What age are your potential readers? What gender? Are they likely to be from a specific geo- graphic location? Do they have special interests?

• Know your competition. Find books similar to yours and read their reviews. See what others like about their books. Check out the author's Amazon author page, their website, and their blog. See where their books are priced. Learn everything you can about your competi- tion. Learn from their successes and their failures.

• Prepare a budget. There are lots of free resources out there, but it is unlikely you will be able to publish a book at no cost whatsoever. Consider these potential costs:

o Editing
o Proofreading
o Cover design
o Formatting
o Printing
o Distribution
o Advertising

• Think about your brand as you act upon your marketing plan. For authors, your brand is your name. Think about what you want people to say about you, and then behave accordingly. Be consistent within your website, blog, author profile, on-line discussion groups, and inter- views. As Warren Buffet once said, "It takes twenty years to build a reputation and five minutes to ruin it."

• And finally, track the results and revise your marketing plan as needed.

MEDIA KIT

Always have a media kit available to send to the media when asked or to hand out at book signings, speaking engagements, conferences, and any other place where there is potential for self-promotion. At a minimum, include the following:

• Book summary
• Press release
• Select book reviews
• Author bio and headshot
• Image of book cover
• Where to buy the book
• Author contact information

CREATE A GOOD PRODUCT

I almost hesitate to include this on the list, but more than once I have been asked to review a fellow author's manuscript or published book, and it violates every writing rule on the books and/or it contains typos. At the very least, I recommend investing in a professional proofreader.

WEBSITE

It is essential for authors to have a website, and for those of you who have never created one, or think you don't have the skills to create one, think again. It's not that hard. I used Yahoo Site Solution to create mine, but there are numerous others available. Just Google "free website design" and you'll see tons of site design tools for free. If you truly can't handle designing your own website, or don't have the time, you can always hire it done. Be prepared to pay a minimum of $1,000 for a very basic site.

Before creating your website, you'll have to get yourself a domain name. Domain registration is cheap and easy. I used Namecheap, but there are many others available. Most web hosts offer domain registration as well. Put thought into the name. There are tips for choosing a good domain name on the Internet such as you'll find on thesitewizrd.com.

You'll also need a web host in order to post your website on the Internet. I used Yahoo, but there are numerous others. My advice is to find one that offers 24/7 tech support. Some are better than others.

Things to include on your website are:

• A "Home" page that welcomes people to your site and gives them an overview of what's inside

• Your bio, including a photo of yourself
• Your contact information
• A synopsis of your book and cover of your book if published
• Testimonials
• Links to other sites you think may be on interest to your audience
• Some sort of "freebie" whether a sample of your work, writing advice, sharing your expertise, links to related sites, etc.
• Where to buy your book
• The right keywords in the page titles, tags, and contents of your page

Promote your website as often as you can. Include the URL on your business cards and stationery (if you use stationery, and if you're under 25, if you even know what stationery is). Include the URL as part of your bio. Put it in your e-mail signature block. Whenever you give someone your contact information, include your website URL.

BLOG

You have to blog nowadays. (If you're reading this article from my website, and you've checked out my photo, you know this statement didn't exactly roll off my tongue.) In my day... well, never mind. Today people blog. They read blogs, and they follow blogs. Blog, blog, blog.

It's relatively easy to create a blog. There are numerous blog templates to choose from. I chose WordPress. It's easy to use and it's clean. For me, there's nothing worse than a cluttered blog where you have to sift through a lot of erroneous stuff looking for what's meaningful to you. Another pet peeve I have is to see typos in blogs. Blogs should be well thought out and proofread. Otherwise, you may lose credibility with your audience.

Most bloggers aren't going to spend time reading or following a blog that doesn't interest them, so the lesson here is to create material that is of interest to those who you want as followers. Sounds like a simple concept, but it really isn't. It takes a lot of thought to get it right. Focus on providing your readers with free worthwhile informational content, even if it means commenting on other peoples' blogs or directing them to other sites. It's okay to have fun, too. Don't be afraid to do something a little crazy once in awhile.

People love freebies, and free eBooks are a great giveaway since they don't cost you anything.

Conducting polls can generate great discussion on your blog. I've seen authors post things like "Choose which cover you like best," "Tell us about your all-time favorite character in a book," and "What makes you keep turning the pages?" You might learn something very valuable in the process.

It's one thing to create and maintain a meaningful blog, but it's quite another thing to draw people to it and then become your followers. Including the right keywords will help. Asking questions can also result in some lively discussions and keep viewers coming back. I saw on one person's blog, "Make me smile today... leave a comment or question."

Don't forget to include other links on your blog. Make it easy for readers to see what else you have to offer, including the link to buy your books.

Blog sites need to be consistently updated with new material. Once to twice weekly appears to be an acceptable frequency. Too few posts and you'll appear stale. Too many may cause an overdose for your audience.

Remember, promoting your books should be secondary on your blog. If you do a good job with the rest of it, book sales will follow.

Like websites, blogs take time to catch on. Don't get discouraged the first year.

AMAZON.COM AUTHOR PAGE

If your book is available on amazon.com (and if it isn't, you're missing out), it behooves you to create an Amazon author page where you can include your bio, photo, a link to your website, blog and twitter page, events, and videos.

SIGNATURE BLOCK

Be sure to include all your links in your e-mail and stationery signature blocks.

BOOKMARKS (not the electronic kind) Bookmarks are an inexpensive way to promote your books. Include on your bookmarks a copy of your book cover, a synopsis, your bio and all your web links. Carry them with you wherever you go and give them away like you would a business card. Pin them to community bulletin boards. Always include one in books you give away. Ask your dentist, hairdresser, or dry cleaners if you can leave a supply in their reception area.

ON-LINE DISCUSSION GROUPS

There are numerous online discussion groups you can join to get advice, give advice, and network with authors, editors, book reviewers and publishers. Three of the most popular venues for discussion groups are Facebook, LinkedIn and Goodreads (see more discussion on each of these down the page). Become an active participant in discussions--the more you interact with fellow members, the more you learn and the more exposure you'll get for your books. Look for successful authors in these groups who have great web pages and/or blogs you can follow and learn from them.

Many groups have separate areas of the site that will allow you to post information about your book. Use these to promote your book, but don't forget to provide feedback on postings from your fellow authors. Not only are you helping them gain exposure, but you will gain some for yourself. These groups are all about helping each other.

FACEBOOK PAGE
Social media sites are a must for authors, and Facebook is by far the largest and most popular. But before you go promoting your book on your Facebook wall, give serious thought to creating a Facebook Page (f/k/a Facebook Fan Page). This will keep your professional posts and other activities separate from your personal ones. Facebook Pages are viewable by anyone, even non-members, so your posts can get significant exposure with the right keywords. One of the great features of the Facebook Page is that when someone 'likes' your page, it gets broadcasted to their contacts, potentially reaching many more people who may be interested in your books.

Post milestones, book launches, interviews, and book signings on your Facebook Page... anything that you deem interesting to your followers and potential book buyers. As long as you keep it interesting, it won't be considered spammy. Strike a good balance for the number of posts. Too few and people will think it's not an active and current site. Too many and people may get annoyed. Be generous with including links, not only links directly related to you, but include other links that may be interesting or helpful to your audience members. Direct your visitors to places they may not otherwise have visited.

It's important to get people to "like" your Facebook Page, as search engines, such as Google, favor Facebook Pages with lots of "likes." One way to get "likes" is when you "like" someone else's Page, ask them if they will return the favor.

Just remember, Facebook is all about creating relationships, whether you're using your personal profile or professional page. It is not advisable to use Facebook strictly as a selling tool. Once you make connections and earn their trust, the sales will come naturally as a side benefit.

LINKEDIN
What Facebook does for social networking, LinkedIn does for business-oriented networking. With more than 50 million members worldwide, LinkedIn provides a vast pool of valuable networkers and potentially buyers for your books. Just as you would create interesting posts for your blog and Facebook Page, you would do the same in LinkedIn. But also like Facebook, you don't want to make your LinkedIn site into a hard sell endeavor. That will just turn people off.

Use LinkedIn for offering interesting articles, making announcements and reaching out for advice and/or offering advice. Increase your visibility by encouraging discussions and comments. Offer freebies. Create contests. Make it fun. Even though it's business, people still like a little fun.

REVIEWS
Book reviews are the best way to promote your book, and while you can pay good money for them, you can also get them for (almost) free. For the cost of a book and postage, you have the opportunity to get great publicity from a good review, and the rewards can be enormous by posting them on your website, your blog and anywhere else you have exposure.

One way to get reviews is on amazon.com. When someone tells you they really enjoyed your book, ask them if they would write a short review on Amazon. A positive book review on Amazon is worth its weight in gold. Potential book buyers read reviews! If you can get ten or more positive reviews, your book looks like a winner for anyone looking to buy it.

You may want to try offering a free book to someone in exchange for a review. Just be cautious who you pick. If it isn't an experienced reviewer, you may get back something you don't want to ever share with anyone. Experienced reviewers know how to highlight the important things you did well and constructively state where the book needs improvement.

It's not easy to get one of the top five book reviewers to review your book, but it's always worth a try. They are Library Journal, Publishers Weekly, Kirkus Reviews and Midwest Book Review. A more comprehensive list may be found at stepbystepselfpublishing.net/reviewer-list.html. Some charge for their services, and others don't.

BRAGMedallion.com is a privately held organization that brings together a large group of readers, both individuals and members of book clubs, located throughout the United States, Canada, and the European Union. BRAG (Book Readers Appreciation Group) states its mission as "recognizing quality on the part of authors who self-publish both print and digital books." Books submitted are read and evaluated by members drawn from its reader group and judged using a proprietary list of criteria, but the single most important criterion they ask their readers to use in judging a book is whether or not they would recommend it to their best friend. Once a book meets this standard of quality from three out of three reviewers, they award it their B.R.A.G. Medallion™. Less than 15% of books submitted receive this honor, so if you submit your book and you become an honoree, you can use it proudly to help promote your book.

Whatever you do, do NOT pay someone to post bogus reviews on Amazon.com or any other site. Not only is this dishonest and less than honorable, but you'd only be fooling yourself about the quality of your writing.

INTERVIEWS
You may be surprised at how easy it is to get interviews that focus on you and your book. Send your press release or other promotional pieces to radio and TV stations, newspapers, newsletters and magazines and ask for an interview. A local ethnic TV station contacted me when they saw the press release for my first novel, "The Coach House," and invited me in for an interview. My book had an ethnic thread running through it, and they thought their viewers would be interested in it. Did I mention they have 500,000 viewers? You'll also find agents, publishers, editors and other authors who include author interviews on their blogs. I ran across several such people in the online discussion groups in which I'm a

member.

BOOK CLUB AND DISCUSSION GROUPS

Book clubs and book discussion groups love to have the author present for their discussions. The tricky part is finding a book club who is interested in your book. Word of mouth may be the best way. Spread the word to your friends you would be willing to participate in a book club discussion.

There are thousands of online book clubs, but since they are online and accessible to anyone, you can be sure they are inundated with requests, so try to be genre-specific in your queries. Here is one book club list book-clubs-resource. com/online/. I am sure there are many others.

BOOK PROMOTION SITES

Launched in 2007, Goodreads is the largest site for readers and book recommendations in the world. They claim to have over 8,900,000 members who have added more than 320,000,000 books to their shelves. Goodreads allows authors to submit their books for consideration.

Here's a list of other book promotion sites.
Authonomy
Bibliophil
Book Buzzr
BookBrowse
Bookhitch
Booksie
Filed By
Jacket Flap
KindleBoards
LibraryThing
Nothing Binding
On Book Talk
SavvyBookWriters
Scribd
Shelfari
Wattpad
WhoWroteThat
WritersNet

LOCAL ESTABLISHMENTS

Write letters to the editor of your local newspapers, newsletters, and trade journals. Call your local radio station and offer to do an interview. Contact your local library and book stores and offer to do a signing or free lecture. Talk to everyone you visit about your book--your dry cleaner, dentist, doctor, and grocer. Look for bulletin boards wherever you go to post information about your website,

blog and books. Make the postings fun and eye-catching.

BUSINESS CARDS

Something as inexpensive and easy as business cards will let others know you're a serious professional writer.

POST CARDS

I live in a 56-story high rise with 482 other residents who are neighbors (of sorts) and potential book buyers. I designed a postcard with a very easy-to-use template from Paper Direct and sent it to all my neighbors. On the front, where the stamp and address label go, I included an image of the front cover of my book, a one-sentence synopsis, and the fact that I'm a local author. On the back, I included a little longer synopsis, where they can find my book, a few promotional sentences from someone who had reviewed my book, and my contact information.

PRESS RELEASES

Press releases get the message out about your book launch, and anyone can write one. Send yours to any media outlet you think will be interested in helping you promote your book - TV and radio stations, newspapers, magazines, newspapers, book stores, book clubs, book discussion groups, book reviewers, etc.

There are templates available such as on PRWeb.com, pressreleasetemplates. net and smallbusinesspr.com for do-it-yourself ones. If you want to engage a service, try mymediainfo.com, cision. com or vocus.com. Muckrack.com is a free service.

TESTIMONIALS

Testimonials can be a great tribute to the story you've written, even if coming from family and friends. Post them on your website and in your blogs.

Here's something fun to try. If your storyline includes something a certain celebrity or group of celebrities could relate to, send a request to their manager or agent asking for a testimonial from the celeb. For example, let's say you've written a story about how a young man pulls himself out from the depths of an impoverished childhood and makes a name for himself in the world. Wouldn't it be a coup if Jay-Z or Jim Carrey (each with a similar story) would endorse your book with a two-sentence testimonial?

TARGET GROUPS

Try connecting with groups or associations who can identify with your protagonist and/or storyline. For example, let's say your protagonist is biracial and has a difficult time fitting in. There are probably hundreds, if not thousands, of people out there who have experienced the same thing and many of them belong to the Association for MultiEthnic Americans (AMEA) or subscribe to Mavin Magazine. On AMEA's website, they list recommended books (fiction and non-fiction) for their members, and Mavin Magazine has an E-Library available for their subscribers. This would be a good opportunity to offer some freebies or a discount for members. Since there's a group out there for just about everything, this avenue is worth pursuing.

I signed up for a Google Alert for the title of my book, "The Coach House." That's when I discovered there are quite a few restaurants around the country and in Europe named The Coach House, and that got me to thinking. I sent each one of them a letter telling them we had something in common and maybe we could do something fun that would benefit us both, like have them hold a drawing (business cards in a fish bowl) where one of the prizes was a copy of my book. In return, I could advertise their restaurant on my website, blog, and Facebook page. Think outside of the box, they say.

FAMILY AND FRIENDS

Don't discount word-of-mouth with family and friends. If all my FB friends re-posted my book announcement, I would reach close to 10,000 more people. That's a lot of potential book buyers.

Florence Osmund earned her master's degree from Lake Forest Graduate School of Management. After more than three decades of experience in corporate America, she retired to write books. Visit her website for substantial new author advice and links to other interesting sites and resources for authors.

Website: https://www.florenceosmund.com

Blog: http://www.florenceosmundbooks. wordpress.com

Article Source: https://EzineArticles. com/expert/Florence_Osmund/1348284

Author Lorenza Fontenot's New Book

Scandalous Jazmynn' is a Psychological Romantic Murder Mystery About a Scandal

Recent release "Scandalous Jazmynn" from Newman Springs Publishing author Lorenza Fontenot is a mysterious thriller containing scandal, murder, and possibly wrongful imprisonment. Jazmynn's life takes an unexpected twist, just when she is graduating college with honors her life becomes full of horrors.

Lorenza Fontenot has completed her new book "Scandalous Jazmynn": a gripping and potent thriller about Jazmynn's life changing for the worse right before finishing college.

"As I look at myself in the mirror, I come to the realization I just might be pretty. I mean my self-confidence is pretty high, but after a few failed dates, I was beginning to wonder if I was loveable. And it dawned on me, am I relationship material? Then I came out with the truth to Dev how I felt about him. I just might be all that and more! I mean, someone actually wants and loves me! I recently bought some makeup to wear for my graduation ceremony. Which I ended up not wearing for lack of knowledge on how to apply it. Well, there will be no need for it now! I have a man! I chuckle to myself. It's still unbelievable."

Published by Newman Springs Publishing, Lorenza Fontenot's climatic tale details Jazmynn's life as it takes a turn for the worse when she graduates from college.

Right before graduation, Jazmynn gets jumped by her date's wife and ends up in the hospital. Jazmynn

Lorenza Fontenot

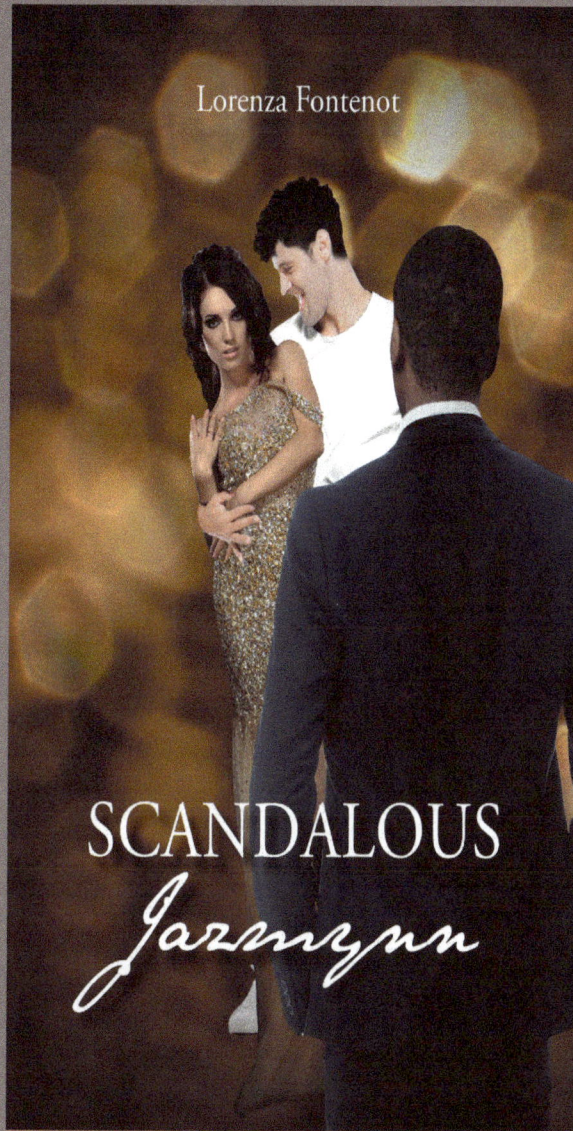

SCANDALOUS
Jazmynn

decides to express her love for Devon after she graduates college. Devon is the man she has had a crush on for years and never expressed her feelings. She takes a risk and goes to Las Vegas to make her confession to Devon.

Unexpectedly, she runs into Peter Williamson, an entrepreneur. Jazmynn's best friend, Janae Carter, and Peter join Jazmynn for a walk in the park. Now, Jazmynn is arrested and put in jail for murder. Readers will find out if Jazmynn is the murderer or if she was framed for a crime she did not commit.

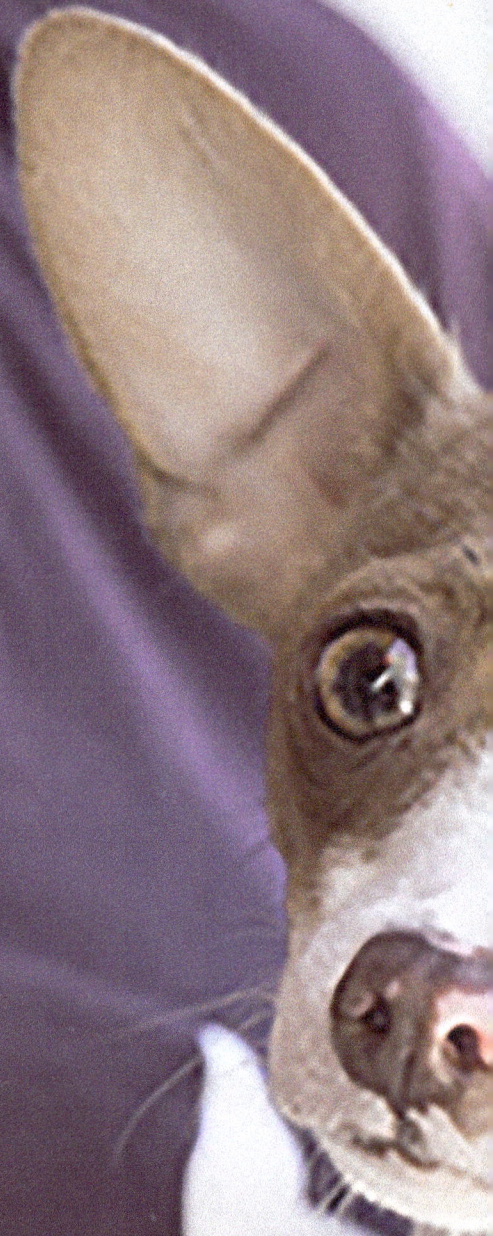

WE WILL NOT TAKE THIS SITTING DOWN

It's time to take a stand for homeless pets. It's time to adopt change. Every day, more than 4,100 dogs and cats are killed in shelters across the country — but **with Best Friends Animal Society leading the way, and your support, we can help our nation's shelters and Save Them All**

SAVE THEM ALL

Award

NYT Bestselling Author Tosca Lee Wins Two International Book Awards for Pandemic Duology

New York Times bestselling author Tosca Lee won two International Book Awards this week—one each for her 2019 pandemic thriller, The Line Between, and its 2019 sequel, A Single Light.

By Mickey Mikkelson

The double win is the latest highlight in a series of award nominations for the duology, which have already won Literary Titan silver (The Line Between) and gold (A Single Light), and finaled for many others including the High Plains Book Awards, the Library of Virginia's People's Choice Awards, Oklahoma Romance Writer's National Readers' Choice Awards (The Line Between), Killer Nashville's Silver Falchion, and Realm Makers Awards (both books). The Line Between was also a Goodreads Choice Awards semifinalist for best mystery/thriller of 2019.

The International Book Awards celebrates excellence in all sections of the publishing industry. Over 2000 entries were submitted to this year's awards.

The Line Between duology centers around 22 year-old main character Wynter Roth, who has just escaped a Midwest cult as a frightening disease begins its spread across the U.S.

The Line Between released January, 2019 from Howard Books/Simon & Schuster. The book's sequel, A Single Light (released September, 2019, Howard Books/Simon & Schuster) comes to paperback August 18. A Single Light is currently on sale for $1.99 in eBook through the end of

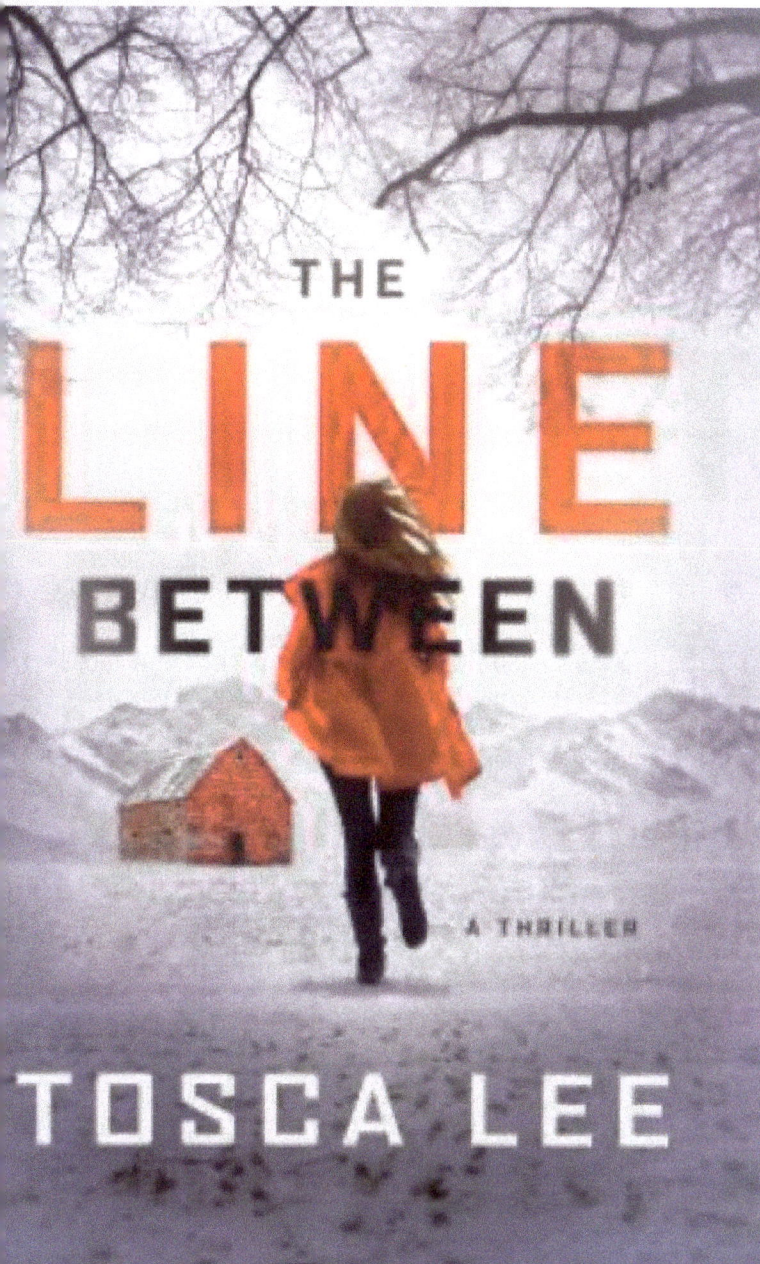

the month.

Watching the news one year after the release of The Line Between, Lee—who has 11 bestselling novels to her credit—calls life "a bit surreal."

The Line Between has been optioned by Radar Pictures (Jumanji) and Ed Burns'
 Marlboro Road Gang Productions (Public Morals) and is in development for
 television as first reported by Deadline Holly-wood: https://bit.ly/32nXQ3I

ABOUT TOSCA LEE

Lee is the multi award-winning, New York Times, and CBA bestselling author of 11 novels including The Progeny, Firstborn, Iscariot, The Legend of Sheba, and The Books of Mortals series with New York Times bestselling author Ted Dekker. Her books have been translated into 17 languages and been optioned for TV and film.
Tosca received her B.A. in English from Smith College. A lifelong world adventure traveler, she lives south of Fremont, Nebraska with her husband and three of four children still at home. To learn more about Tosca, please visit ToscaLee.com

'A Journey from Fat to Flat'

A Revealing New Book by A'Cora Berry About Overcoming Sexual Abuse and Obesity

Today, 11 years before her 50th birthday, she's the picture of health at an ideal weight. "I have tons of energy for my daughters, and my husband is so proud of me," says A'Cora, who recently become a United States citizen as well as completing a screenplay.

RANCHO PALOS VERDES, Calif.

Author, filmmaker and entrepreneur A'Cora Berry says she remembers enduring many cruel blows in her 39 years. The murder of her father when she was 5, sexual abuse at 7, and a horrific traffic accident that left her husband a quadriplegic when she was 34. And through most of her life, there was another foe -- food. In her latest book, "A Journey from Fat to Flat" -- my story of overcoming childhood sexual abuse and struggling with being overweight, A'Cora shares her secrets for losing weight and getting fit for life.

For A'Cora, founder of MacBe Entertainment specializing in producing films that inspire people and propel acting careers, "A Journey from Fat to Flat" begins while driving with her husband to visit family members. "I was in my early 30s and just casually mentioned wanting to be fit by 50," she remembers. "Well, my husband expressed some skepticism and wondered why I wasn't interested in getting healthy sooner -- like now? That was something I really wasn't prepared to hear, but it was exactly what I needed to hear."

So, A'Cora made the commitment to start transforming her life. "We have two daughters, Mackenzie and Bella, and the thought of not being around for them was all of the motivation I needed," she said. "I started slowly by giving up two of my favs -- chocolate and flavored coffee creamer. In fact, my husband used to tease me about having a little coffee with my creamer."

In addition to eliminating a number of offending foods and sweets, she also embraced a vegetarian lifestyle along with exercise, including weight training. "And instead of starting way too fast and burning out a few days later, I took my time. I ate in moderation and kept track of everything. It took about four years to reach my goal weight. And because my program is based on lasting lifestyle changes and moderation, I've been able to keep it off."

Today, 11 years before her 50th birthday, she's the picture of health at an ideal weight. "I have tons of energy for my daughters, and my husband is so proud of me," says A'Cora, who recently become a United States citizen as well as completing a screenplay.

"Fat to Flat" is filled with practical techniques she personally used to lose weight, including meditation. "I'm still thrilled every time I look down and its flat," she laughs. "The days of covering up are over. Above all, I never forget that adversity will not define me. I came to this world to fulfill my purpose."

And that also means helping others lose weight and be healthy. To get a copy of A'Cora's "A Journey from Fat to Flat" -- my story of overcoming childhood sexual abuse and struggling with being overweight, which also includes a progress chart, go to acoraberry.com or amazon.com.

A'Cora Berry

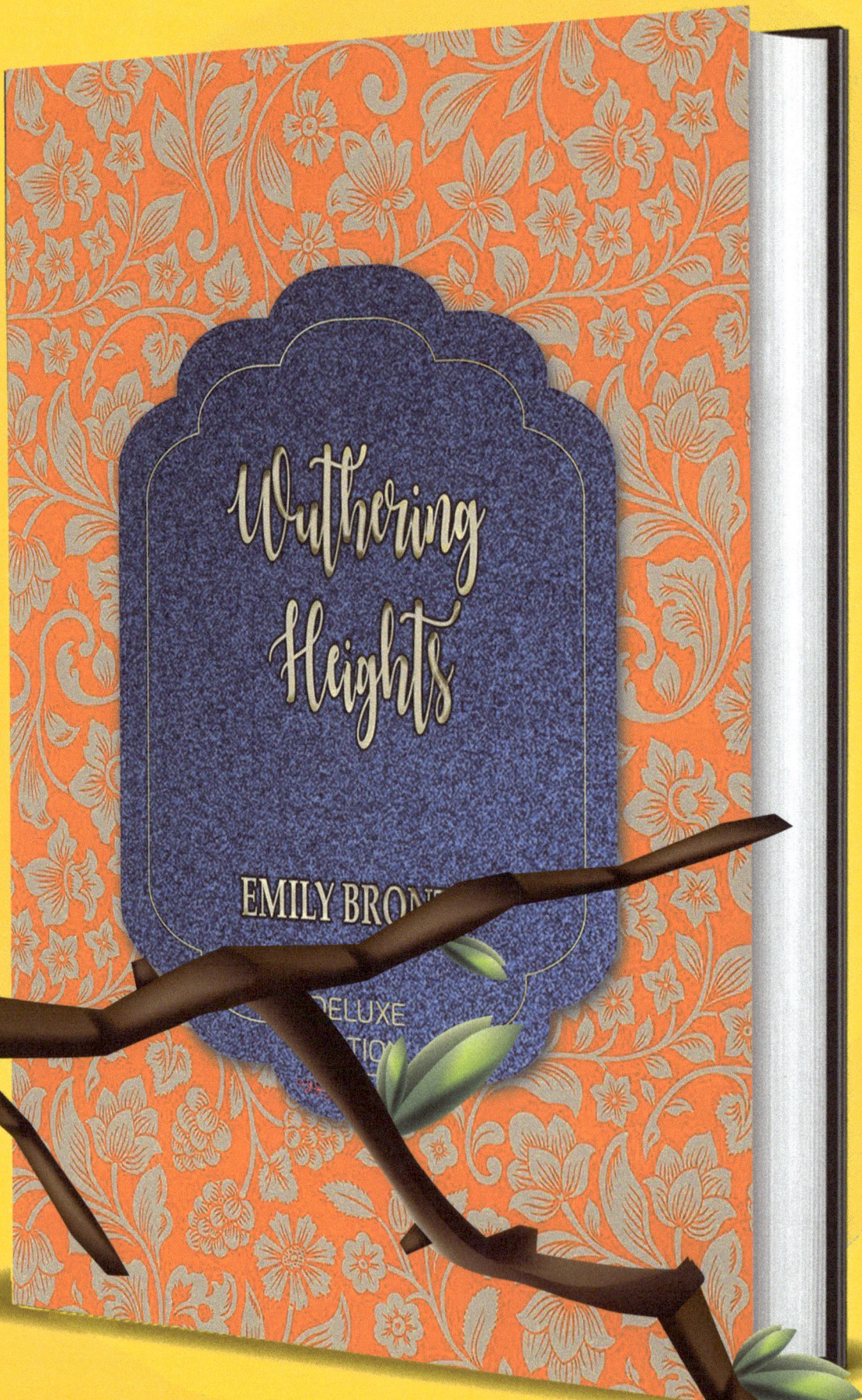

Wuthering Heights

EMILY BRONTË

DELUXE

Deluxe Edition

Collected from the Guardiand's and
the Telegraph's "the 100 greatest novels of all time" list.

Preserved the original format whilst repairing
imperfections present in the aged copy.

See the complete list at
iboo.com

New

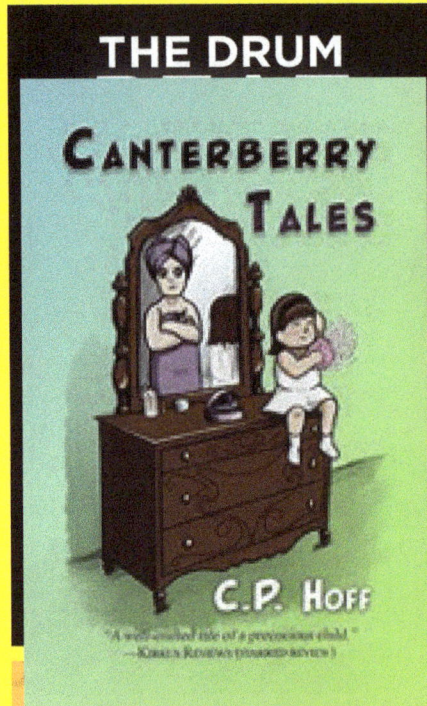

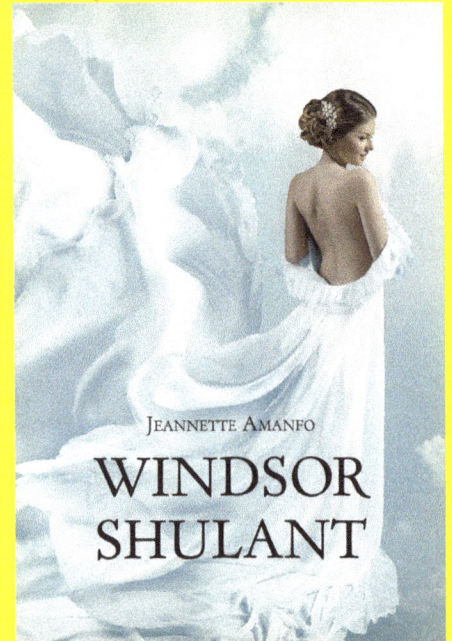

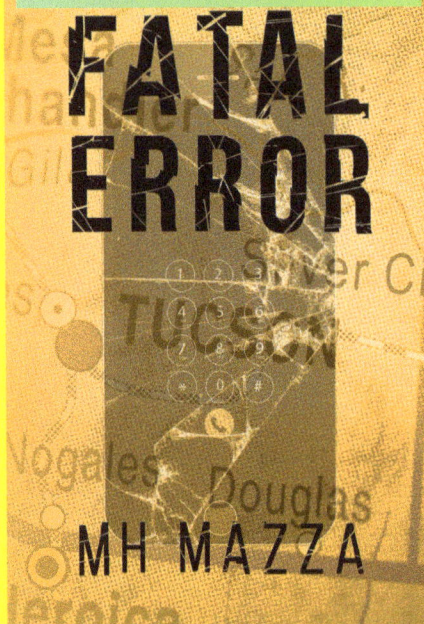

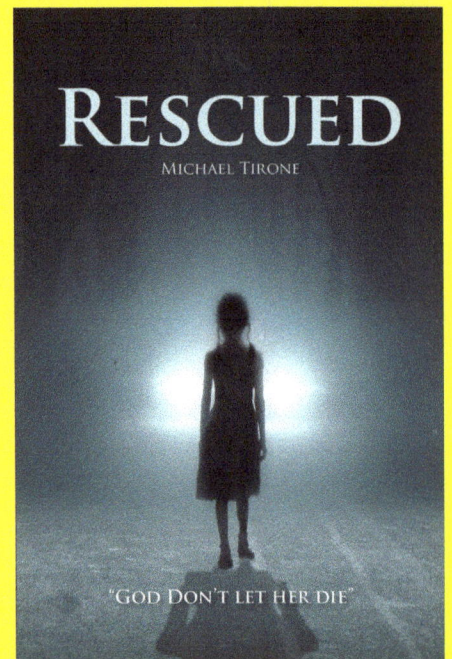

New

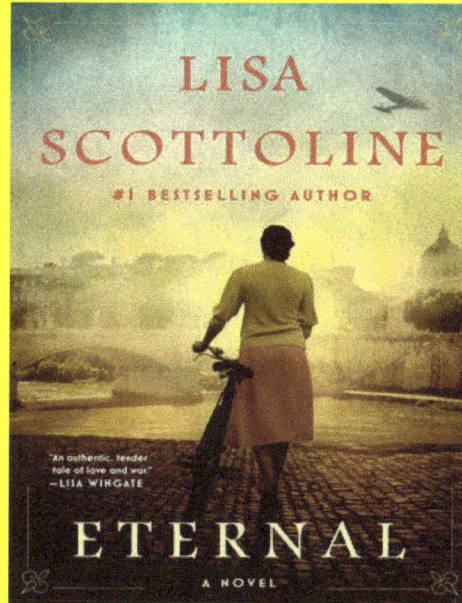

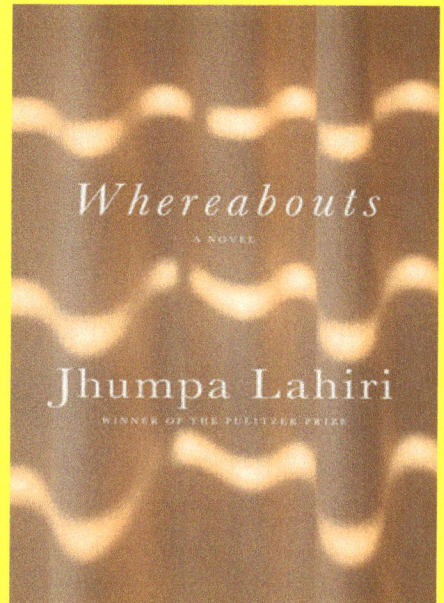

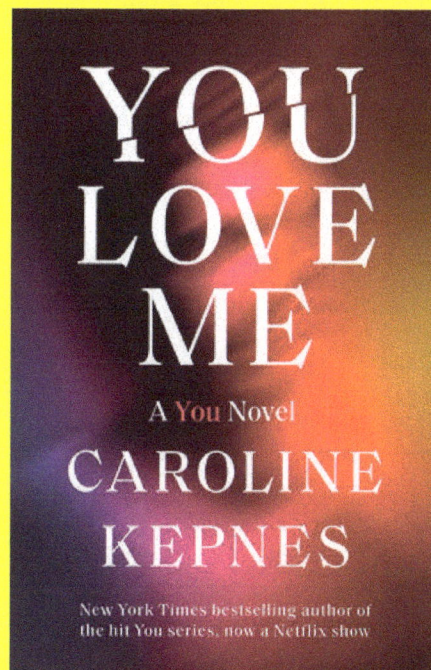

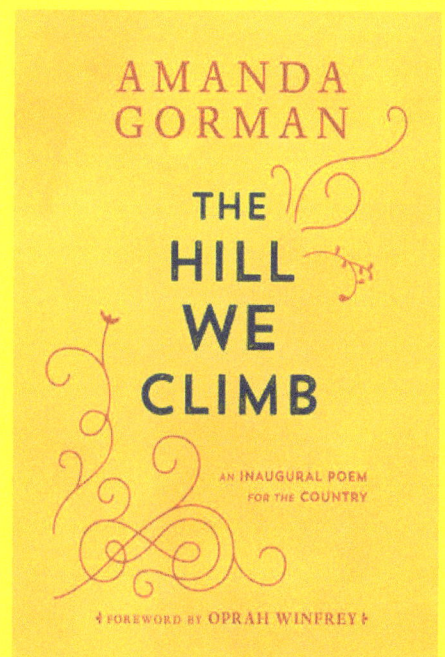

Ranveig Elvebakk, MD's New Book 'THE ORIGINS of ILLNESS: Health and Illness in the Quantum Era' is a Brilliant Read That Links the Body's Well-Being to the Environment

Ranveig Elvebakk, MD, a Scandinavian-born medical doctor, and fitness advocate, has completed her most recent book "THE ORIGINS OF ILLNESS: Health and Illness in the Quantum Era": a potent analysis on how the physical environment and the human body affect each other. It studies the body's response to the changing planet and allows readers to understand this relationship in order to come to a symbiosis, subsequently preventing illnesses and diseases.

SAN FRANCISCO, April 15, 2021 - Ranveig Elvebakk, MD, a Scandinavian-born medical doctor, and fitness advocate, has completed her most recent book "THE ORIGINS OF ILLNESS: Health and Illness in the Quantum Era": a potent analysis on how the physical environment and the human body affect each other. It studies the body's response to the changing planet and allows readers to understand this relationship in order to come to a symbiosis, subsequently preventing illnesses and diseases. Elvebakk writes, "Illnesses, be they physical or mental, can be seen as imbalances between our forces and those of the universe. Understanding this relationship gives us the ability to change processes and reverse illness. This is confirmed by the mainstream medical literature and clinical observations. The book updates medicine to incorporate this untapped scientific information."

Thoughtful, systematic and very timely, this book is fundamental to transforming our relationship with our health and that of the planet.

Published by Fulton Books, Ranveig Elvebakk, MD's book elucidates on the of-

THE ORIGINS OF ILLNESS

Ranveig Elvebakk, MD

OF

ILLNESS

Health and Illness in the Quantum Era

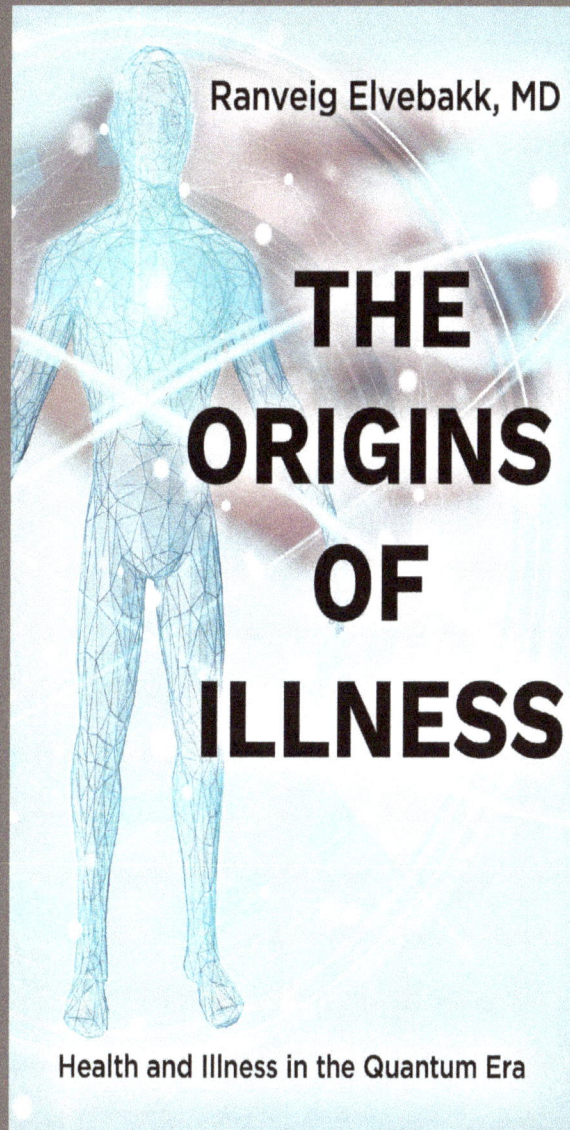

ten-neglected link between bodily health and the health of the environment.

Readers who wish to experience this informative work can purchase "THE ORIGINS OF ILLNESS: Health and Illness in the Quantum Era" at bookstores everywhere, or online at the Apple iTunes store, Amazon, Google Play or Barnes and Noble.

New

NEW & NOTEWORTHY

NEW & NOTEWORTHY

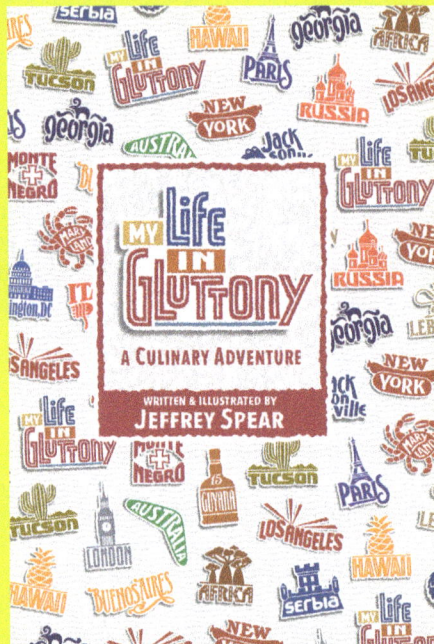

My Life in Gluttony: A Culinary Adventure — Written & Illustrated by Jeffrey Spear

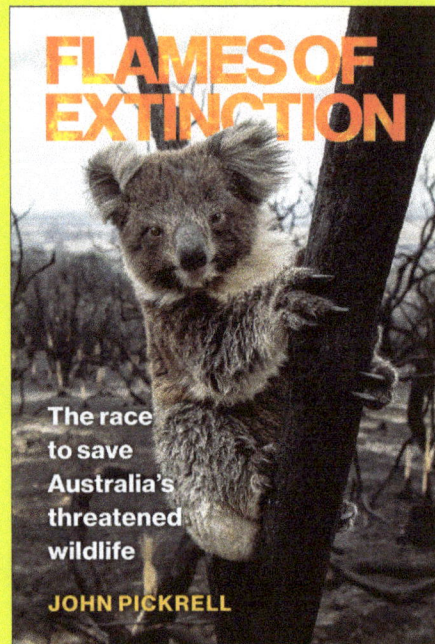

FLAMES OF EXTINCTION — The race to save Australia's threatened wildlife — JOHN PICKRELL

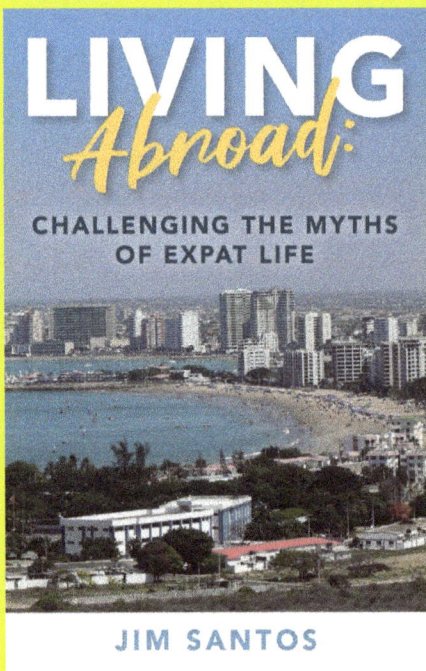

LIVING Abroad: CHALLENGING THE MYTHS OF EXPAT LIFE — JIM SANTOS

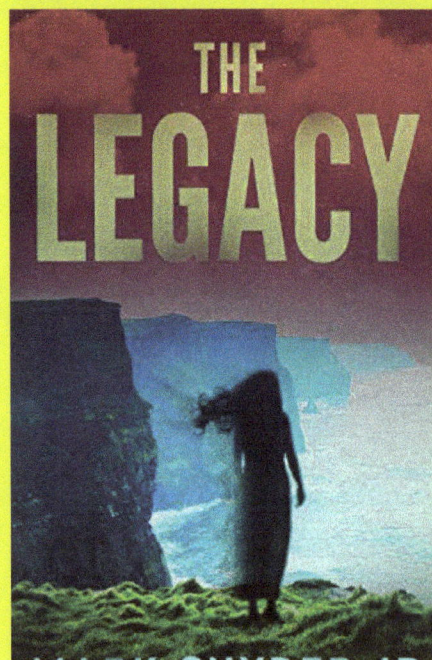

THE LEGACY — MARK SNYDER JR.

Avaiable at bookstores everywhere, or online at the Apple iBooks Store, Amazon, or Barnes & Noble.

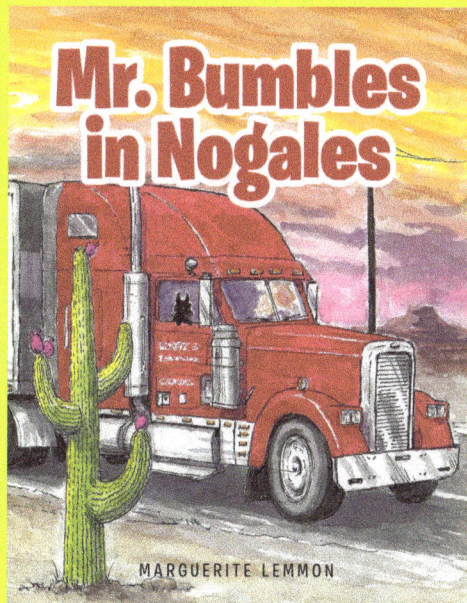
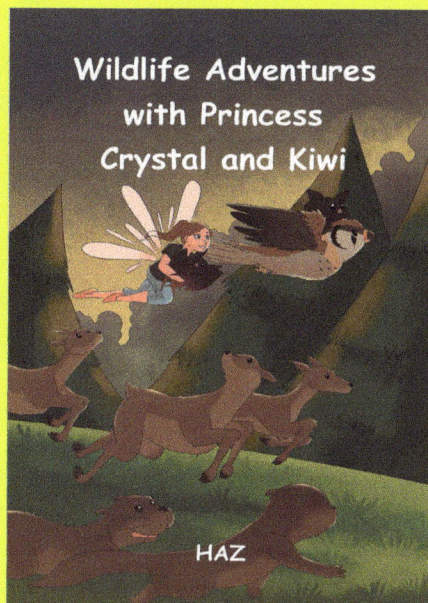
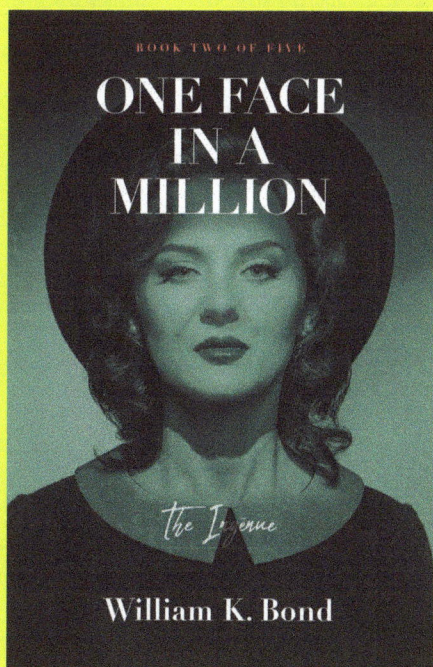
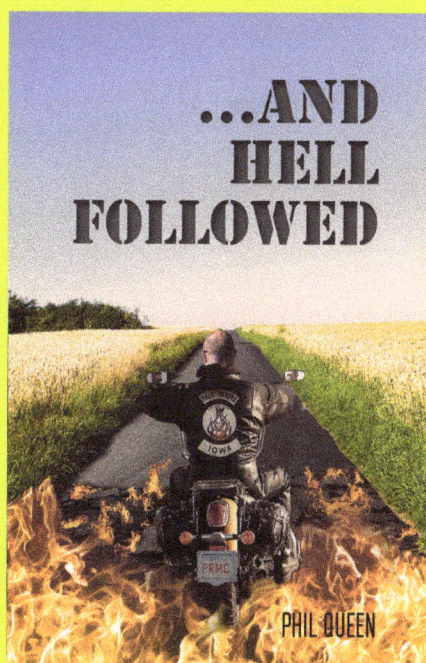

BOOK

Health

Are You S***ting Me?! How to Survive, Thrive and Transform Through Colorectal Cancer, written by Oils & Spoils blogger Kim Mullins, is available for pre-order through 1 a.m., April 22. Are You S***ting Me?! is an irreverent, yet informational play-by-play of how to navigate, understand and plan for surviving, thriving and transforming through illness.

Author of Are You S*ting Me?! How to Survive, Thrive and Transform Through Colorectal Cancer**

Health

Personal Experience of Colorectal Cancer is an Irreverent, Cheeky Tail of Surviving, Thriving and Transforming Through Illness

Are You S***ting Me?! How to Survive, Thrive and Transform Through Colorectal Cancer, written by Oils & Spoils blogger Kim Mullins, is available for pre-order through 1 a.m., April 22. Are You S***ting Me?! is an irreverent, yet informational play-by-play of how to navigate, understand and plan for surviving, thriving and transforming through illness.

"Personal experiences of colorectal cancer are few and far between, and the subject itself seems more taboo than talking about sex. Not that cancer is sexy, butt seriously, we need to talk about it. See what I did there?" the book's author, Kim Harris Mullins, said.

In the United States, colorectal cancer cases are on the rise, and the larges demographic for this recent uptick are millennials. According to the American Cancer Society:

Millennials born around 1990 are two times more likely to develop colon cancer and four times more likely to develop rectal cancer compared to young adults in the 1950s.
The rate of colorectal cancer has

been steadily increasing among adults younger than 50 since the mid-1980s. Conversely, incidences of colorectal cancers have dropped for those over age 50. Young adults are more likely to be diagnosed with a late stage of colorectal cancer due to the perception by both young adults and doctors that they are not likely to develop the disease.
Deaths from colorectal cancer for people younger than age 55 have increased 2 percent every year from 2007 to 2016.
Colorectal cancer is the third leading cause of cancer-related deaths in men and women.
Colorectal cancer is the second most common cause of cancer-related deaths in men and women combined.
The lifetime risk for developing colorectal cancer is 1 in 23 for men and 1 in 25 for women.
The number of new colorectal cancer cases estimated for 2020 is 147,950.
104,610 new cases of colon cancer
43,340 new cases of rectal cancer
Regardless of the "type" of cancer you might have, this book promotes:

Awareness of the rise of colorectal cancer and what you can do

for prevention
The importance of early screening
How to advocate for your own health before, during, and after cancer Unique organizational tools to help you through your journey Reframing your brain and other coping techniques
Thriving after cancer, including living with an ostomy and paying it forward A s***load of funny anecdotes (hey, humor helps, right?)

"During my cancer journey, I went through radiation, chemo, and surgery, which resulted in a permanent colostomy bag, post-op chemo, and external lupus caused by the chemo. Don't even get me started on jokes around being a 'bag' lady," Mullins said. "Having cancer was the scariest time of my life, and I wish I'd had someone to talk to openly about what I was experiencing.

Are You S***ting Me?! is the inspirational, informational, but oh-so-hilarious guide I wish I'd had before, during, and after my struggle."

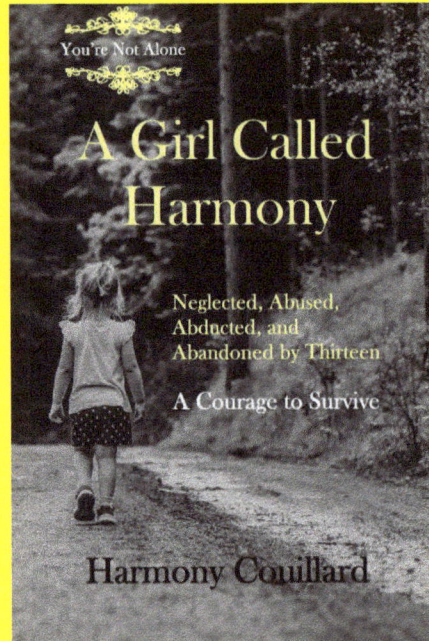

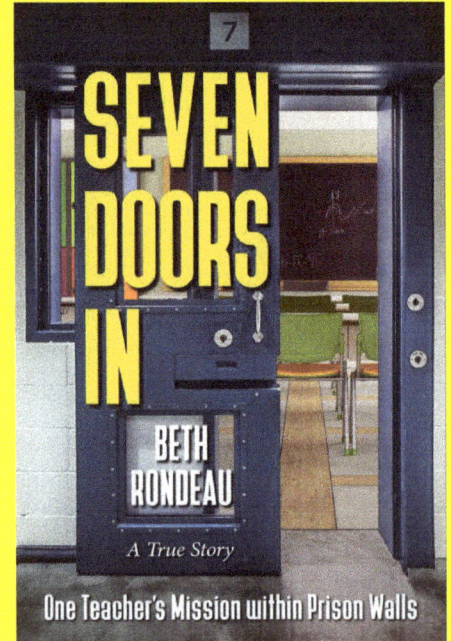

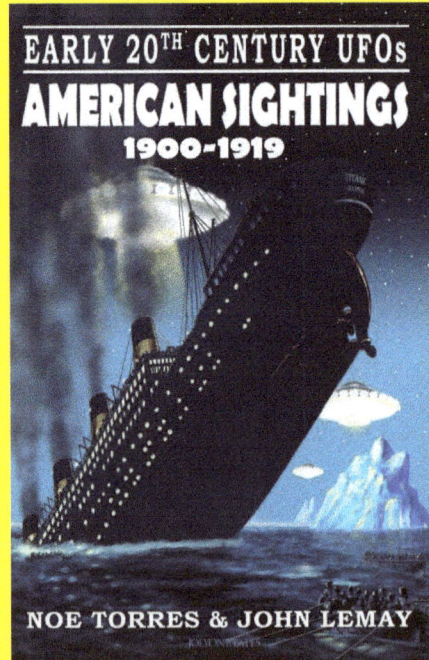

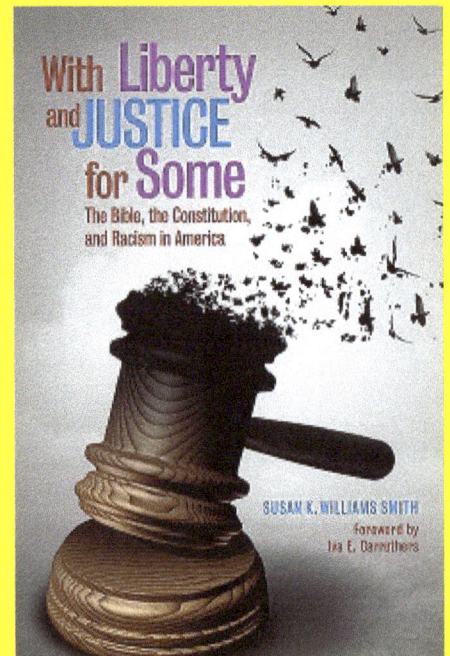

New

NEW & NOTEWORTHY

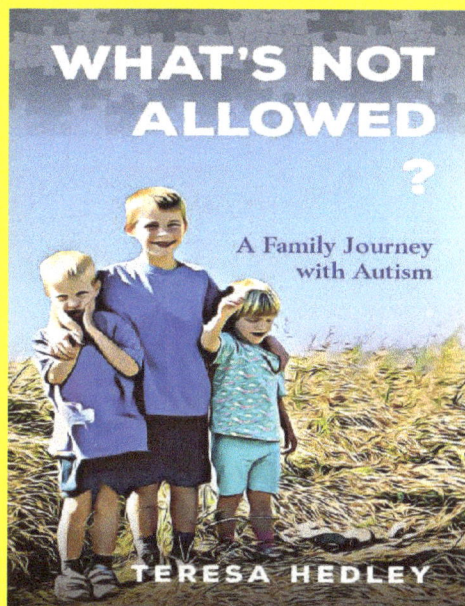

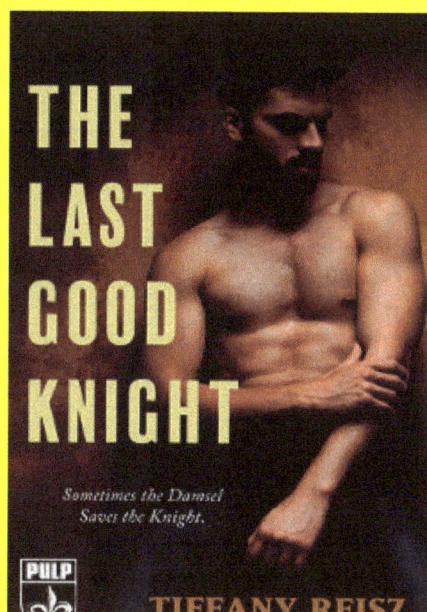

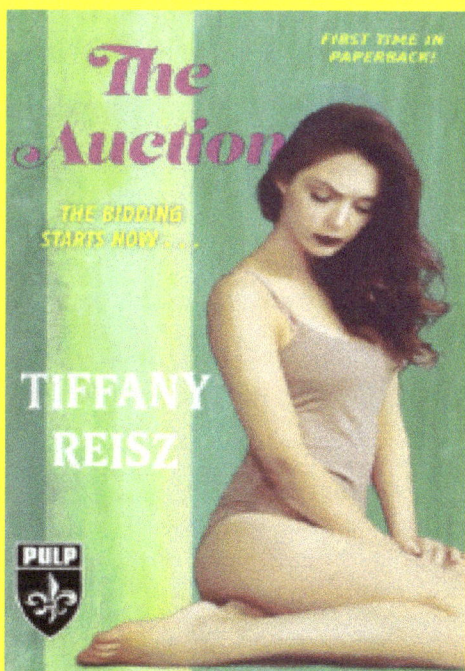

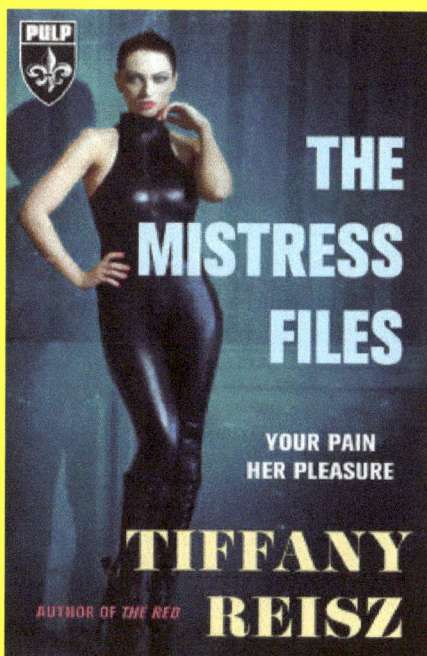

WHAT'S NOT ALLOWED?
A Family Journey with Autism
TERESA HEDLEY

THE LAST GOOD KNIGHT
Sometimes the Damsel Saves the Knight.
PULP
TIFFANY REISZ

FIRST TIME IN PAPERBACK!
The Auction
THE BIDDING STARTS NOW...
TIFFANY REISZ
PULP

PULP
THE MISTRESS FILES
YOUR PAIN HER PLEASURE
TIFFANY REISZ
AUTHOR OF *THE RED*

Avaiable at bookstores everywhere, or online at the Apple iBooks Store, Amazon, or Barnes & Noble.

The Wizard of Oz As an Allegory

Dorothy is the main character who represents the average American who travels the "yellow brick road" which signifies the gold standard to reach the Emerald City - the greenback dollar to find the "Wizard".

BY HARRINGTON A LACKEY

When Frank Baum wrote the American classic, "The Wonderful Wizard of Oz" in 1900 it was a popular book for young people to read. Later in 1939, the story became immortalized as a movie, shot partly in black and white and color, starring Judy Garland, as a young farm girl in Kansas who hits her head in a tornado, and dreams she's landed in a mythical world of munchkins, witches, a scarecrow, a tinman and a lion who journey to meet Oz, a powerful magician. However, based on a recent MSN article, "Why pennies still exist and other money trivia" by Andrew Lisa, there is "overwhelming scholarly evidence" that the story is an allegory of the American economic status at the end of the 19th century, known as "Populism".

In the 1890s, Populism referred to the Populist movement that grew out of the financial insecurity that the average American, mainly farmers who earned a meager income suffered from failing crops, falling prices, and true fear of financial favor. In other words, Populists wanted economic power for the common people who earned a scant amount from their jobs. They wanted money to be based on the "gold standard" so that their currency could be exchanged for gold.

The context of the Populist movement probably never would have been connected as a parable of the "Wonderful Wizard of Oz" until author and historian Henry M. Littlefield published an article in 1964 in the "American Quarterly", in which he clearly explains the characters' symbolic meaning in the Populist movement. Dorothy is the main character who represents the average American who travels the "yellow brick road" which signifies the gold standard to reach the Emerald City - the greenback dollar to find the "Wizard".

Dorothy meets some friends along the way, who have needs that only the Wizard can offer them. For example, the Scarecrow represents the average American farmer who claims to need a brain. The brain is a metaphor for education from universities. The Tinman is the industrial worker who builds items made of steel. He needs a heart since the manufacturing industry operates with dehumanized, indifferent workers. The Cowardly Lion who is the politician, Williams Jennings Bryan, who according to Populists, was afraid to run against President William McKinley, who is the Wizard. McKinley is the top American politician who seems wise and benevolent but is really an evil, conman who doesn't know what he is doing. Nevertheless, the Wizard gives the Lion courage.

Other characters in the Wizard of Oz include the Wicked Witch, who is the monetary system, killed by Dorothy-the average middle American who had the power to kill the witch if she only believed in herself. In the book, Dorothy wears silver slippers, instead of "Ruby slippers" in the movie. The silver slippers represent the "anti-inflation" free-silver movement, in which silver was used to mint coins, circulating among the American people.

In considering the "Wonderful Wizard of Oz" as a symbol or allegory for the early Popular Movement, it's easy to view that the story is really about money and politics.

Article Source: https://EzineArticles. com/expert/Harrington_A_Lackey/1594833

Source: EzineArticles

The Art of Making Art!

BY NISHA SINGH

Hi everyone!! Welcome to another #ThoughtfulThursday with me, Nysha.

Today, I thought to share my process before a painting goes into the making, I hope it helps you in some way to get you into the zone for creating any kind of art, whether it's painting, drawing, making music, making a video, etc. This process isn't in anyway a rule-book, each artist has his/her own way and process to get into the creative zone.

Let's get started:

Basic Idea: This part of the whole process is a random one, sometimes it just clicks, I might get an inspiration from a concept I recently read about, or a picture I looked at online, or a combination of colors I saw somewhere, I don't have a fixed pattern, an idea can originate from anywhere if you keep your eyes and mind open at all times. That's when I either make a note in my phone, or sketch a basic thing in sketchbook if I have it with me at the time.

1501867067174

Collecting References: Whether to use references or not has been a debatable topic since a really long time now, I like to see it this way, well, the idea can be implemented with or without references depending on what you are making, using references does not mean you copy it blindly, it just means to take inspiration, sometimes it's important to use referenced, as for example when you are drawing a tree, you might not be able to look at a tree where you are drawing it, so you would naturally use a reference picture of a tree, whereas when it comes to abstract, you need not use references. Once, I have an idea, I tend to collect some references and use them all for sometimes I end up using none, it's too unpredictable for me.

My Creative Space: One of the most important things for me is to have a soothing space where I feel absolutely at ease and am free to create whatever I envision. I usually, light a candle, or probably an incense stick (I love those), put on some great music (what kind? totally depends on my mood), then I make some green tea or coffee, once I have my

environment all bright and shiny, that's when the real work begins.

Execution: So, as you've known by now, making art seems a like a quick process rather it's much more than just picking up the canvas and start putting colors onto, it is rather a longer process which takes time & patience. After all this, I quickly make up my mind about which colors to use on my piece, and the background according to the painting, if I am making a portrait, background is something I struggle with quite often so I make sure to plan it ahead to avoid my misery later on.

And the painting begins...

my process pic 1

P.S: This Lord Ganesha Painting and prints are available online on my website.

I try to upload daily updates on my Instagram, you can follow me @nyshaartstudio

Website - http://www.nyshaartstudio.com

43

www.ingramcontent.com/pod-product-compliance
Lightning Source LLC
Chambersburg PA
CBHW052348210326
41597CB00037B/6300